THE ARCTIC

EUROPE

ASIA

THE HIMALAYAS

AFRICA

MADAGASCAR

AUSTRALIA

W9-BKS-947

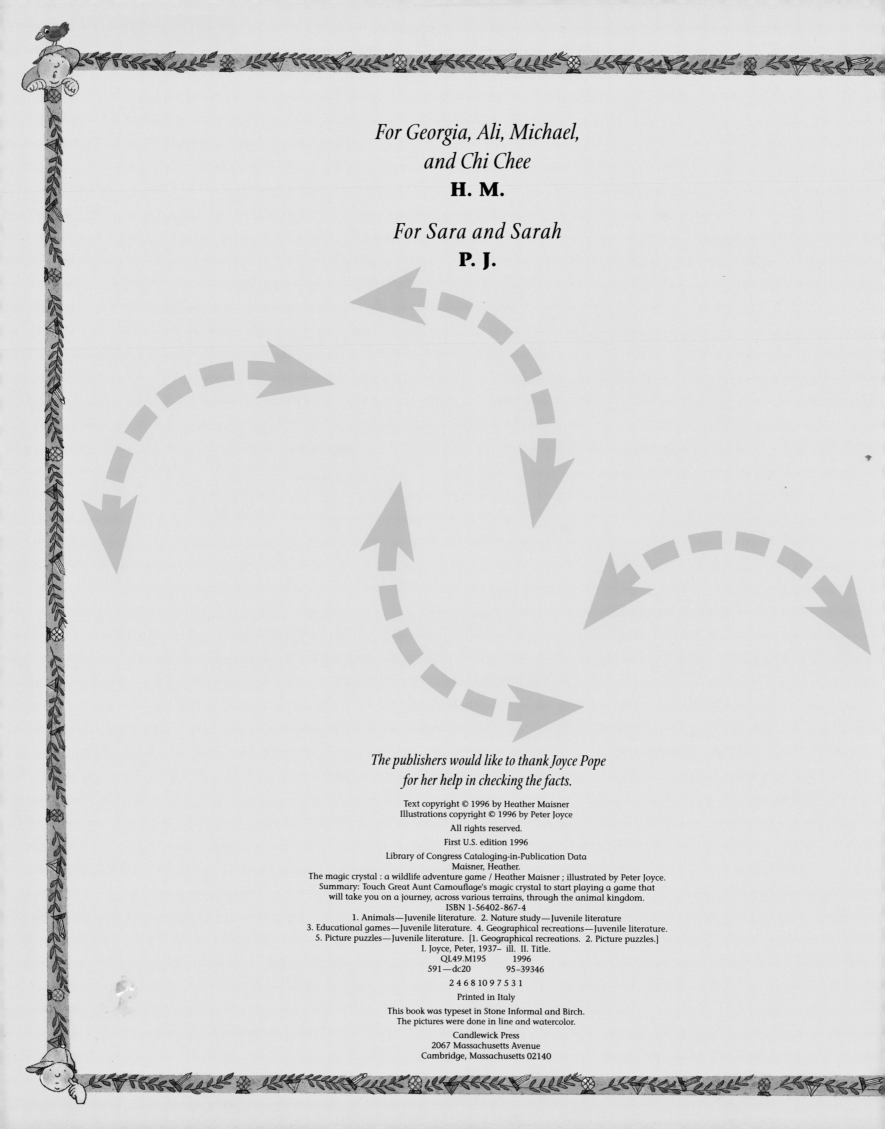

For Georgia, Ali, Michael,
and Chi Chee
H. M.

For Sara and Sarah
P. J.

The publishers would like to thank Joyce Pope
for her help in checking the facts.

Text copyright © 1996 by Heather Maisner
Illustrations copyright © 1996 by Peter Joyce

All rights reserved.

First U.S. edition 1996

Library of Congress Cataloging-in-Publication Data
Maisner, Heather.
The magic crystal : a wildlife adventure game / Heather Maisner ; illustrated by Peter Joyce.
Summary: Touch Great Aunt Camouflage's magic crystal to start playing a game that
will take you on a journey, across various terrains, through the animal kingdom.
ISBN 1-56402-867-4
1. Animals—Juvenile literature. 2. Nature study—Juvenile literature
3. Educational games—Juvenile literature. 4. Geographical recreations—Juvenile literature.
5. Picture puzzles—Juvenile literature. [1. Geographical recreations. 2. Picture puzzles.]
I. Joyce, Peter, 1937– ill. II. Title.
QL49.M195   1996
591—dc20   95–39346

2 4 6 8 10 9 7 5 3 1

Printed in Italy

This book was typeset in Stone Informal and Birch.
The pictures were done in line and watercolor.

Candlewick Press
2067 Massachusetts Avenue
Cambridge, Massachusetts 02140

THE MAGIC CRYSTAL

HEATHER MAISNER
ILLUSTRATED BY **PETER JOYCE**

CANDLEWICK PRESS
CAMBRIDGE, MASSACHUSETTS

ANIMAL ZONE CHART

Read the instructions on the next page before you start to play.

	PAGES	ZONES	EXCITING EXPEDITIONS
⊠ White	6 and 7	HOME	All games begin and end here!
Blue	8 and 9	TUNDRA	WINTER · SUMMER
Red	10 and 11	CONIFEROUS FOREST	IN THE FOREST · BY THE LAKE
Yellow	12 and 13	DECIDUOUS FOREST	AMONG THE TREES · IN THE SOIL
Blue	14 and 15	OCEAN	SURFACE WATERS · IN THE DEPTHS
Blue	16 and 17	GRASSLANDS	THE SAVANNA · A WATER HOLE
Green	18 and 19	AUSTRALIA	THE OUTBACK · THE BUSH
Red	20 and 21	SWAMP	ABOVE THE SWAMP · AT THE SWAMP
Green	22 and 23	DESERT	MORNING SUN · MOONLIT NIGHT
Red	24 and 25	ISLANDS	GALÁPAGOS ISLANDS · MADAGASCAR
Yellow	26 and 27	RAIN FOREST	UP IN THE TREES · UNDER THE BRANCHES
Green	28 and 29	MOUNTAINS	THE HIMALAYAS · THE ANDES

Lost belongings

jacket
straw hat
dress
socks
swimsuit
flippers
leggings
pants
barrette
walking shoes
cardigan

shorts
umbrella
rain hat
sunglasses
sandals
rain boots
goggles
cap
T-shirt
vest
scarf

Lost animal notes: Where did Great Aunt Camouflage see these animals?

a frog that carries babies in its mouth

a duckbill platypus

springtails

a crocodile with a baby on its head

the world's fastest animal

a grizzly bear

a Gila monster

a poison arrow frog

two remoras

the abominable snowman

a crowd of lemmings

blue-footed boobies

6

Your Great Aunt Camouflage, a famous zoologist, has sent you
this note and a wonderful magic crystal. Touch it and
you will be sent on an exciting journey through
the animal kingdom.

HOW TO BEGIN YOUR JOURNEY

☞ Touch the magic crystal, say "**zoomazoo**," and turn the page.
Choose Exciting Expedition 1 or Exciting Expedition 2. Read the clues
and follow the route through the scene.

☞ When you reach the end of the route, look for the magic crystal,
hiding nearby. Be alert! Wherever it goes, the magic crystal changes
its color and sometimes its shape too.

Here are three examples:

☞ When you find the magic crystal, return to the Animal
Zone Chart on page 6. Find the matching crystal and turn
to the pages listed beside it. Choose Exciting Expedition
1 or 2 and set off again.

☞ Continue on your journey until the magic crystal turns
white again and leads you back home.

☞ Be sure to look out for me, too. I'm hiding in three places
somewhere in the animal kingdom. And keep a lookout for
my **22 lost belongings** listed on page 6.

☞ Play with the magic crystal as often as you like. Each
game will be different—some long, some short.

Have fun and don't get lost,

Great Aunt Camouflage

P.S. I've lost some of my **animal notes**. Can you tell me where
I saw the animals listed on page 6?

Touch the
magic crystal!
Say "zoomazoo!"

WINTER

It is winter in the tundra—the cold, flat land below the Arctic Ocean that rings the North Pole. The ground is frozen. It is -58°F and a fierce wind is blowing.

◄-- THE ROUTE --►

☞ Find **SNOWY OWLS** swooping through the sky. Their coats stay white all year round and feathers on their feet and toes protect them from icy winds and snow.

☞ Cold? Join three **MUSK OXEN** standing together to keep warm. Under their long coats is a layer of wool, as soft and light as cashmere.

☞ Step forward to the white **ARCTIC FOX** chasing a hare. When resting, it fluffs out its fur to trap air, helping it keep warm. It also has fur on the soles of its feet.

☞ Tired? Join the birds in their white winter feathers. They are **WILLOW PTARMIGAN** and they dig hollows in snowdrifts for shelter from icy winds. In summer their feathers will change to speckled brown.

☞ Say hello to two black **RAVENS**, then help the **ARCTIC HARE**, digging in the snow. A thick white winter coat keeps it safe and warm.

☞ Move on to the two **POLAR BEARS**, waiting beside a crack in the ice. They have long, dense fur all over their bodies, apart from the nose, and a layer of fat up to 4 in. thick.

☞ Feeling frozen? Crawl into the den and snuggle up beside the female **POLAR BEAR** and her two young cubs.

☞ SEEK THE MAGIC CRYSTAL

SUMMER

It's summer in the tundra—the vast, treeless land that surrounds the North Pole. For a few months, the days are long, the sun doesn't set, and birds and other animals arrive from the south.

◄-- THE ROUTE --►

☞ Find two **WOLVERINES** on the left. They look like bears but are related to weasels. They are also called gluttons since they eat so much.

☞ Cross the stream but avoid the black cloud of **MOSQUITOES** and tiny **MIDGES**. The females all suck blood.

☞ Pass two tall birds called **CRANES** and join small **LEMMINGS** hurrying along. The lemmings feel overcrowded and have decided to emigrate at once. Nothing can stop them.

☞ Step across to the **ARCTIC TERNS**— small birds with black caps and red bills. They have flown here from Antarctica, 12,500 miles away, and will fly back before winter comes. Many birds come here to nest in the summer.

☞ Hot and sticky? Splash around with the **OLDSQUAW**. Then look up at the **SNOW GEESE**, flying in formation. Each goose flies in the slipstream of the one in front. This helps them conserve energy as they fly.

☞ Feeling tired? Ask the last **REINDEER** in the herd for a ride. They are also called caribou and have traveled north from their winter homes in the forest. Here in the tundra they will find food and give birth to their young.

☞ **SEEK THE MAGIC CRYSTAL**

IN THE FOREST

You are in Canada in the vast coniferous forest that forms a belt south of the frozen tundra. Dense trees block out the sun and the ground is covered with pine needles and moss.

◄-- THE ROUTE --►

☞ Find the **GRIZZLY BEAR**. The white tips on its soft, thick fur can make it look "grizzled," or gray. It has a good sense of smell and can run up to 30 mph.

☞ Climb the tree with the slow, clumsy **PORCUPINE**. Go carefully and do not touch it. The quills may be loose and could stick under your skin.

☞ Look left and see the **FLYING SQUIRREL** about to land on a tree. When it jumps, the skin between its feet and body makes a parachute that it can glide on for 100 to 130 ft.

☞ Move across to the bird feeding five young chicks. She's a **BLACK-CAPPED CHICKADEE**, and a member of the titmouse family.

☞ Say hello to the **WOODPECKER**, then land between two leaping **MARTENS**. They belong to the weasel family, but live mostly in the trees, jumping from branch to branch.

☞ Go down to the wildcat chasing a **SNOWSHOE HARE**. It is a **LYNX**, whose enormous feet are covered in fur.

☞ Join the line of tiny **SHREWS**, holding on to their mother by their tails. Shrews are among the smallest of all the mammals.

☞ Now step across to two beetles on a branch. These **PINE WEEVILS** use their long snouts to pierce the bark of the tree and lay their eggs.

☞ SEEK THE MAGIC CRYSTAL

BY THE LAKE

You are by a lake in the vast coniferous forest of Canada. Many animals come here out of the dark forest to splash around in the water and look for food in the sunlight.

◄-- THE ROUTE --►

☞ Find the **MOOSE** wading through the lake, eating water plants. This tall forest animal is a good swimmer and a fast runner.

☞ Skim across the water with the **DRAGONFLY**, the fastest flying insect. Dragonflies were living on Earth before the dinosaurs.

☞ Look up at the **OSPREY** with a fish between its claws. This bird of prey, which lives near water throughout the world, has rough spiky feet to help grip slippery fish.

☞ *Splash!* **GOLDENEYE** ducklings are jumping from a tree nest into the lake to follow their mother. This is how they learn to swim.

☞ Want to play follow-the-leader? Join two **OTTERS** sliding down the muddy bank. They are among the few mammals, like humans and dolphins, that make up their own games.

☞ Now leap with the **FROGS**. They are amphibians: they can live both on land and in water.

☞ See the brown animal standing in a hollow tree stump on the right? It's a **MINK** with a beautiful silky coat. Don't go too close; it stinks.

☞ Lend a hand to the **BEAVERS** using logs, sticks, and mud to build a "lodge"—a safe house in the water. They use strong sharp teeth to gnaw down trees. When in danger, they slap their broad, flat tails on the water as a warning.

☞ SEEK THE MAGIC CRYSTAL

AMONG THE TREES

You are in a deciduous forest in Europe. Deciduous comes from the Latin for "to fall" and each autumn leaves fall from the deciduous trees.

◄-- THE ROUTE --►

☞ Find the **WILD BOAR** with babies, grubbing up roots with their snouts. They move in noisy groups and can run very fast.

☞ See **SWALLOWS** flying after insects, then help the colorful **JAY** collect acorns. It stores each acorn in a separate place up to 1.5 miles away.

☞ Overtake the **BEECH MARTEN** running up a tree trunk and help the **EDIBLE DORMOUSE** get away. The ancient Romans loved to fatten these large dormice and eat them.

☞ Slide down past the **LIZARD** to the **BADGER** gathering dried grass for its underground home. Don't upset it. It can be quite fierce.

☞ Move on to the **MOLE** peeping out of the hole. It feels safest in its rambling underground tunnels.

☞ Join the **HEDGEHOG** snuffling along. It has over 5,000 spines, and when frightened, it rolls itself into a ball.

☞ Now step back to help the **TOAD**, which has puffed itself up to try to look bigger. It has just seen a **GRASS SNAKE**, and snakes can dislocate their jaws to stretch their mouths very wide around their prey.

☞ SEEK THE MAGIC CRYSTAL

IN THE SOIL

You are moving through the soil of a deciduous forest in Europe. The moist floor of fallen leaves is home to thousands of mini beasts.

◄-- THE ROUTE --►

☞ Wriggle by the pink **EARTHWORM** on a leaf on the left. It swallows soil as it moves, digesting the good parts and forcing the rest out behind.

☞ Join the **ANTS** clambering over a log. They are carrying food to millions of other ants who live in giant nests underground.

☞ Move on to the **SNAIL**—a mollusk with a soft body and a hard shell. It moves slowly, at one inch a minute, eating plants with its tongue, which is as rough as sandpaper.

☞ Say hello to the **LADYBUGS**, then spring up with the tiny **SPRINGTAILS**. These insectlike creatures have no wings but use their forked tails to jump. They have been on Earth for 380 million years.

☞ Race past the **NUT WEEVIL**, piercing a nut with its long snout, and overtake the trail of **WOODLICE**. They are the only close relatives of the crab family to live on land.

☞ Kick up a leg with the **CENTIPEDE**. It has up to 20 pairs of legs.

☞ Look out! Two **STAG BEETLES** are fighting, using their antlerlike jaws to grab and hold.

☞ Flit past the striped **HOVER FLIES**. They hover up, down, and sideways. Land beside the **CRANE FLY**.

☞ **SEEK THE MAGIC CRYSTAL**

SURFACE WATERS

You are swimming through the sea, which covers over 70 percent of the planet. In these surface waters, warmed by the sun, many animals live and hunt for food.

←-- THE ROUTE --→

☞ Find the **JELLYFISH**. Beware of its long tentacles—they can sting. It has no bones and moves in jerks, pumping water in and out of its umbrella-shaped body.

☞ Swim across to the large fish flapping its fins gracefully, like a huge butterfly. This **MANTA RAY**, with eyes on top of its head and mouth underneath, is also known as the devilfish and is a flattened cousin of the shark.

☞ Interested in magic? Hitch a ride on the manta's tummy with two small **REMORAS**, said to have magical powers. They have disks on their head for clinging to the manta and sometimes they cling to sharks.

☞ Look up at the **ALBATROSS**, an ocean-going bird that spends most of its life at sea, then leap into the air with the **DOLPHINS**. They are mammals who live only in water.

☞ Follow four **FLYING FISH**, leaping together for safety, then dive down and join the **BLUE MARLIN** with a pointed snout. Swim fast. It moves at up to 50 mph.

☞ See that fish with a large head like a hammer and eyes at each side? It is a **HAMMERHEAD SHARK**. Ask it why it looks like this. Nobody knows.

☞ Quick! Dart left into the crowd of **SILVERSIDES**, swimming in a shoal for safety. There can be millions of fish in one shoal. Ask them if they have a leader.

☞ **SEEK THE MAGIC CRYSTAL**

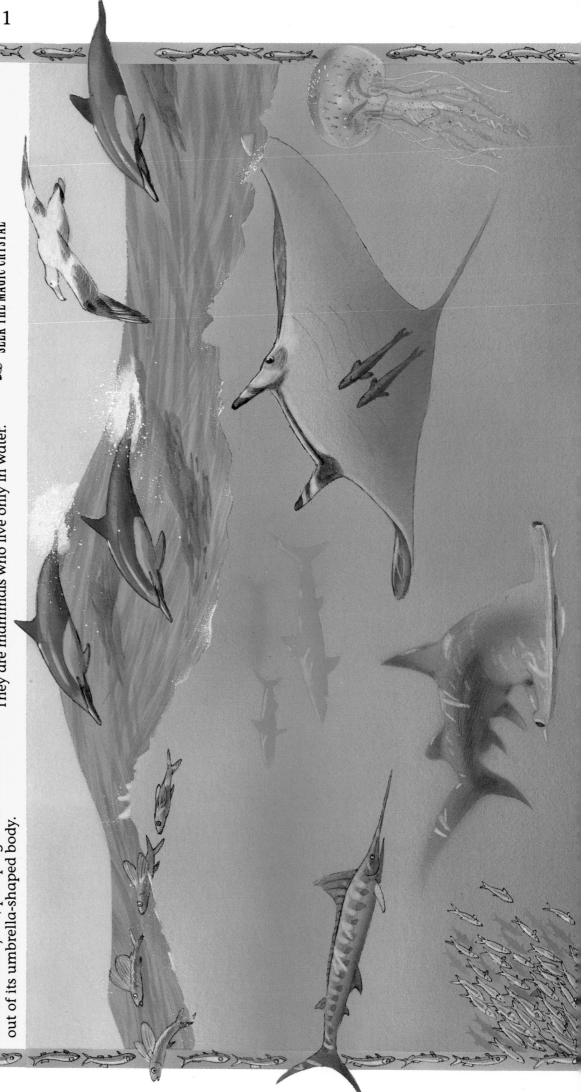

IN THE DEPTHS

You are in the cold, dark depths of the ocean, where there is no sunlight and the water is near freezing. Tons of water press down on you.

◄-- THE ROUTE --►

☞ Find the crowd of nine small **SQUID** with large eyes for seeing in the dark. They are marine invertebrates—animals without backbones—and they move by pumping water in and out of their bodies.

☞ Swim left beside four **GRENADIERS**, or rat-tails, with large heads and long whiplike tails. They have glands that light up in the darkness to see and be seen.

☞ Dive under the two **DRAGONFISH** with rows of lights and teeth like fangs. Their mouths and bodies can stretch to eat creatures bigger than themselves.

☞ Tired? Ride on the enormous **SPERM WHALE**, the whale that dives down the deepest. Whales are mammals whose ancient relatives once lived on land. Now they live only in the sea, where they can stay underwater for up to two hours without breathing.

☞ See that small fish below with a light on its head and a gaping mouth with needlelike teeth? It is an **ANGLERFISH** and the light attracts its prey.

☞ Duck under the giant **SQUID** fighting to escape from the whale. It is one of the fastest animals in the sea and moves up to 40 mph by jet propulsion.

☞ Greet small **HATCHET FISH**, swimming with open mouths. Then join the two red **DEEP-SEA PRAWNS**. Many crustaceans—animals with hard shells like these—live in the dark depths.

☞ **SEEK THE MAGIC CRYSTAL**

THE SAVANNA

You are in the savanna, the vast grasslands of Africa. Many of the world's largest mammals live here.

◄-- THE ROUTE --►

☞ Find four monkeys grooming each other. They are **BABOONS**, who can climb trees but prefer to live on the ground. They move in troops and all look after each other.

☞ Skip between the **ELEPHANTS**, the largest land animals. Their trunk is an extra-long lip and nose. They use it to pick up food, stroke and smack babies, and follow scents.

☞ Beware! A spotted **CHEETAH** is watching from a branch. This cat, the fastest animal in the world, can run up to 60 mph over short distances.

☞ Duck away from the **VULTURE** and hide among the herd of antelope. These **IMPALA** are munching grass. They chew their cud like cows. Many different antelope live here in the grasslands.

☞ Tired? Rest beside the lazy **LION** in a tree. Then reach up with the **GIRAFFE**, stretching out its long tongue to munch leaves that no other animal can reach from the ground.

☞ Jump down and run forward to the gray **AARDVARK** sniffing with its long snout. Its name means "earth pig."

☞ Hungry? Join the small red bird looking out for insects from the back of the large **BUSTARD**. This **BEE-EATER** enjoys having a ride.

☞ SEEK THE MAGIC CRYSTAL

A WATER HOLE

You are at a water hole in the savanna grasslands of Africa. In the long dry season animals search for water to drink and to keep cool in.

◀-- THE ROUTE --▶

☞ Find five **OSTRICHES** running. They are the largest birds in the world. They have lost the ability to fly but can run up to 45 mph.

☞ Stop and face the snorting **RHINOCEROS**, whose sharp horns are made of hair. It leaves piles of dung to mark territory and paths.

☞ Look up at majestic **FISH EAGLES** catching fish, then join dazzling **ZEBRAS**, who can run as fast as horses. Ask them what their stripes are for; no one is sure but each zebra has a different pattern on its coat.

☞ Move between the line of long-faced **WILDEBEESTS**, also known as gnu. Then say hello to four **BUFFALO** with large curved horns. These wild cattle love to wade in the water.

☞ Can you see birds standing on the buffalo? The two white birds are **CATTLE EGRETS**. The small bird is an **OXPECKER** and it is eating ticks.

☞ Hot and sticky? Wallow in the water with the **HIPPOPOTAMUSES**. Their name means "river horse" and they must stay in water by day to avoid sunburn and protect their skin.

☞ Dance around with the **STORK**, then swim forward to the **PANGOLIN** stretching out its wormlike tongue to drink. It has scales for armor.

☞ SEEK THE MAGIC CRYSTAL

THE OUTBACK

You are in the outback, the desert grassland of Australia. Many of the world's marsupials —mammals with pouches for their babies—live only in this area.

◄-- THE ROUTE --►

☞ Follow large birds running. They are **EMUS**, who have lost the ability to fly but can run up to 30 mph.

☞ Hurry past two **DINGOS**—wild dogs—standing beside **TERMITE MOUNDS** that look like tombstones. The mounds are homes to huge families of termites and their queen.

☞ Hungry? Climb up to the **HONEY POSSUM** hanging by her grasping tail. She has a pouch for her babies and feeds on pollen and nectar.

☞ Jump down past the **ECHIDNA** —spiny anteater—who looks like a hedgehog, and land by the **HAIRY-NOSED WOMBAT** peering over a rock. This marsupial digs burrows, chewing through roots like a rodent.

☞ Can you hear angry hissing? It's the **FRILL-NECKED LIZARD**, opening its frill to frighten enemies.

☞ Now step across to the tiny marsupial **MOUSE** and watch two dragonlike creatures fighting. These giant lizards, called **GOANNA**, have snakelike forked tongues.

☞ Snuggle up with the **KANGAROO** and her baby, which is called a **JOEY**. Then splash around with the green **BUDGERIGARS**—tiny parrots who fly in flocks to confuse their enemies.

☞ SEEK THE MAGIC CRYSTAL

THE BUSH

You are in the woodlands of Australia. Many animals live here that do not live anywhere else in the world.

◄-- THE ROUTE --►

☞ Find the **DUCKBILL PLATYPUS** by the water. This mammal has a furry body with a duck's beak and webbed feet. It feeds its young on milk but lays eggs like a bird.

☞ Move forward to the **HERCULES MOTH**, the largest moth in the world with a wingspan up to 11 in. Then join the **BRUSHTAIL POSSUM** with a baby on its back. This marsupial—mammal with a pouch for its babies—can leap through trees like a monkey.

☞ Pass the small marsupial **CAT** crouching in the branches, and sit with the **TREE KANGAROO** above. It can jump on the ground but prefers to leap through the trees.

☞ Can you see three animals like teddy bears? They are not bears but marsupials called **KOALAS**.

☞ Look out! Here come **FLYING FOXES**—large bats with wingspans up to 5 ft. Move left and sit between the white **CUSCUS** and the laughing bird called a **KOOKABURRA**.

☞ Glide along with the **SUGAR GLIDER** on the left and land beside the **LYREBIRD** with its tail spread wide. Move forward to the tiny **LONG-NOSED POTOROO**, standing to look at an insect.

☞ Hungry? Join the banded **NUMBAT** sniffing the ground for food. Its tongue is half as long as its body.

☞ SEEK THE MAGIC CRYSTAL

ABOVE THE SWAMP

You are above a hot, steamy swamp in Asia, where many animals live among the twisted mangrove trunks and go fishing for food.

◄-- THE ROUTE --►

☞ Hide among the trees with the **TIGER** in its striped coat. This large wildcat is an excellent swimmer and comes to the swamp looking for food.

☞ Climb straight up and then leap left with the **FLYING LIZARD**, who can glide up to 65 ft. Land beside the **FISH OWL**. It has scales on its feet for catching slippery fish.

☞ Fly down with the **TREE SNAKE**. This one is known as the "flying snake." It can stretch its body and glide down to the ground.

☞ Hungry? Pass large **WEAVER ANTS** on the left, weaving leaves together with fine silk, then ask the spotted **FISHING CAT** to share its meal. It is the only member of the cat family to live primarily on fish.

☞ Hot? Dip in the water then climb up the bank with the ancient-looking **WATER MONITOR**. This large lizard flicks its forked tongue in and out like a snake, as many lizards do.

☞ Climb up the branch and sit beside the monkey called a **CRAB-EATING MACAQUE**. It has learned to fish for crabs.

☞ Wave to the **FLYING FROG** on the right and climb up to the two colorful **ATLAS MOTHS**. They are among the biggest moths in the world.

☞ SEEK THE MAGIC CRYSTAL

AT THE SWAMP

You are by a swamp in Asia, where the river meets the sea. Animals from land, sea, and river live here.

◀-- THE ROUTE --▶

☞ Find the **CROCODILE** who has tossed a baby onto its head. It carries babies in its mouth for safety. Crocodiles like this have been on Earth for 200 million years.

☞ Go left to the **CRAB-EATING FROG,** then dance across the mud with the six **MANGROVE CRABS.** Thousands of crabs live in these muddy waters. When the tide comes in, they hide in holes so they won't be swept away.

☞ See three strange brown flat shapes with long tails? They are called **HORSESHOE CRABS** and are also known as "living fossils," because they have looked the same for 200 million years.

☞ Say hello to three **MUDSKIPPERS** watching their friend skim over the ground. These fish can move on land and use their fins like limbs to climb.

☞ Skip right to the **HERMIT CRAB,** peeping out from a borrowed shell. Then scuttle forward to the **FIDDLER CRAB** holding up one huge claw.

☞ Hot and sticky? Jump into the water, pass the **SEA SNAKE,** and stop beside the two **DUGONGS,** or sea cows. These large, peaceful mammals live in the water, feeding on sea plants.

☞ Hungry? Help the **ARCHER FISH** shoot jets of water at an insect to knock it off a leaf and eat it.

☞ **SEEK THE MAGIC CRYSTAL**

MORNING SUN

It is early morning in the Arizona desert in the United States. Daytime creatures are on the move before the sun becomes too hot.

◄-- THE ROUTE --►

☞ Find the **GILA WOODPECKER** carving a hole for a nest in a giant saguaro cactus. Its eggs will be safe in here and cactus spines will frighten away enemies.

☞ Wave to the tiny **ELF OWL** above, peering from an abandoned woodpecker's nest. It is one of the smallest owls in the world.

☞ Look up at the **TURKEY VULTURE** sitting on a cactus. It can see for miles around.

☞ Say hello to the **ROADRUNNER** sprinting after a lizard. This bird is related to the cuckoo and can run up to 25 mph, using its tail for balance.

☞ Step forward to the **COYOTE**, panting and sitting by a stone. Its pale fur reflects the sun and panting helps it lower its body temperature.

☞ Look down the burrow at the **KIT FOX** resting, then step across to the **DESERT TORTOISE** nibbling cactus flowers. Its large shell is for protection and to help it keep cool.

☞ Tired? Join the **CHUCKWALLA**—a lizard—lying on a hot rock. Soon it will slip into a crack to cool down. When in danger, it inflates so that it can't be pulled out.

☞ Now, before the desert heat overpowers you, leap down and join the **KANGAROO RAT**, asleep in a cool underground chamber. It has gathered a store of seeds for food.

☞ **SEEK THE MAGIC CRYSTAL**

22

MOONLIT NIGHT

It is night in the Arizona desert in the United States, where the ground is cool, but not yet cold, and night animals are on the move.

◄-- THE ROUTE --►

☞ Find the **KIT FOX** on the right, starting to dig a burrow. Thick hair in its ears keeps out sand as it digs.

☞ Skip past the **SPOTTED SKUNK** doing a handstand. Go carefully! It thinks you are an enemy and is about to spray you in the eyes with stinky liquid from under its tail.

☞ Oops! Here comes a **SIDEWINDER**, the fastest of the rattlesnakes. It moves sideways in loops at 2.5 mph, touching the hot sand as little as possible.

☞ Join the **JACKRABBITS** chasing each other around a cactus. Look at their long ears! They give off body heat, which helps them keep cool.

☞ Now run in a line with the wild pigs. They are **PECCARY** and have let out an odor to warn the herd.

☞ Look up at **WESTERN BATS** chasing night insects. In one night they can eat half their weight in insects.

☞ Say hello to the **BOBCAT** on the left. Oh! Wait a moment. It is squirting urine to mark its territory.

☞ Smile as you pass the huge **GILA MONSTER** in front of a rock. It is one of the only two poisonous lizards in the world, but it is very shy and only uses its poison for defense.

☞ The temperature has dropped. Cuddle up with the three **ROCK SQUIRRELS**, safe and warm underground. For part of the summer, they often "estivate"—go to sleep without eating or drinking.

☞ **SEEK THE MAGIC CRYSTAL**

GALÁPAGOS ISLANDS

These volcanic islands off South America are home to many animals that do not live anywhere else in the world.

◄-- THE ROUTE --►

☞ Find the male **FRIGATE BIRD** with a red sac like a football beneath his beak. He is hoping to attract a mate. These birds steal food from other birds, like pirates of the skies.

☞ Say hello to the **MARINE IGUANAS**—big lizards basking in the sun. They are the only lizards that go into the sea, where they feed on seaweed.

☞ Hungry? Join the red **SALLY LIGHTFOOT CRABS** picking off tasty ticks from an iguana's back.

☞ Dance around with **BLUE-FOOTED BOOBIES**, then help the small bird using a cactus spine to dig up insects. It is a **WOODPECKER FINCH**. Thirteen different kinds of finch live on these islands and are not found anywhere else in the world.

☞ Pass the **GALÁPAGOS SNAKE** and the **PENGUINS** splashing around, and climb up to the short-winged bird on a rock. It is a flightless **CORMORANT**. Here, where it has no enemies, it has lost the ability to fly.

☞ Look up at the long-winged **ALBATROSS**—who spends years at sea without touching land—then join the **GIANT TORTOISES** moving along. The Spanish word for tortoise is *galápago* and the islands are named after these ancient-looking reptiles.

☞ SEEK THE MAGIC CRYSTAL

MADAGASCAR

You are on an island off the southeast coast of Africa—a home to animals not found in other parts of the world.

◄-- THE ROUTE --►

☞ Find two **RING-TAILED LEMURS** with tails raised, prepared for a "stink fight." They are related to monkeys and do not live in any other country.

☞ Climb up and say hello to the green lizard. It is a **GECKO** and has climbing pads on its feet to help grip smooth tree trunks.

☞ Move left to the small gray animal with a bushy tail. It is a lemur called an **AYE-AYE**. It cracks bark with its teeth and hooks insects with one extra-long finger.

☞ Climb up to greet the large white lemur called a **SIFAKA**, then rest beside two black-and-white **RUFFED LEMURS**. Lemur means "ghost," perhaps because some come out only at night.

☞ Jump past the **BAT** and land beside the **CHAMELEON**, the lizard with a curled tail. Sometimes it changes color and can't be seen.

☞ Hungry? Leap down to the brown **FOSSA** at the base of a tree. Then help the red-and-black **SCARAB BEETLE** collect dung. It rolls each piece along then buries it to eat later.

☞ Now run to the right with the tiny striped **TENREC**. This little mammal is related to the shrew.

☞ **SEEK THE MAGIC CRYSTAL**

UP IN THE TREES

You are in South America, high in the treetops of the Amazon jungle, the world's largest rain forest. Join in the hoots and shrieks of the animals as they swing through the trees like acrobats.

<-- THE ROUTE -->

☞ Find three bearded red monkeys called **HOWLERS**, with their mouths wide open. Don't go too close; you might be deafened. Their voices carry several miles across the dense forest.

☞ Hang beside the large **SPIDER MONKEY**, which holds on to branches using its tail like a fifth limb. It can even use its tail to pick up fruit and leaves to eat.

☞ Chat with the **TOUCAN**, the bird with the enormous bright beak. Ask it why its beak is so big. Nobody really knows the answer.

☞ Look up at the fierce **HARPY EAGLE** above you. Beware! It has strong legs, toes, and talons like all birds of prey.

☞ Jump down past the small gray **KINKAJOU** and flit beside two blue **MORPHO BUTTERFLIES**. They are the biggest butterflies in the Amazon, with wingspans of 8 in. Millions of insects swarm in this hot, wet jungle.

☞ Pass the **OCELOT**—a small cat—moving daintily along a branch, and swing through the trees with five tiny **TAMARIN MONKEYS** above. Go carefully! They run around in noisy gangs and sometimes miss their footing.

☞ Swing past the green **TREE FROG** with bulging eyes and land beside the large lizard. It is an **IGUANA**. Don't go too near; it might lash out with its strong tail.

☞ Feeling tired? Climb up and rest beside the **SLOTH**, hanging upside down with its baby. It can stay completely still for up to 18 hours a day, and its fur grows down from its belly so that the rain can run off easily.

☞ SEEK THE MAGIC CRYSTAL

UNDER THE BRANCHES

You are in South America in the Amazon rain forest. It is hot and humid beneath the towering trees. Water drips from the leaves and there is no sun or wind to dry them.

← -- THE ROUTE -- →

☞ Find the long green **TREE BOA** curled around a tree trunk. This snake wraps its body around its prey and swallows it whole, but takes so long to digest its food that it may not eat again for months.

☞ Hungry? Join the **GIANT ANTEATER** standing with its pointed snout near a termite's mound. It is one of the few mammals without teeth but it can push out its sticky tongue up to 25 in. and trap up to 30,000 insects a day.

☞ Find the red-and-blue **STRAWBERRY POISON ARROW FROG** sitting on a leaf at the right. It is one of the most poisonous animals in the world and toxins from its skin are used to make poison arrows.

☞ Itchy from the mosquitoes? Run to the water with three brown **CAPYBARAS**, the largest rodents in the world. They can be 4 ft long and they have partly webbed feet for swimming.

☞ Overtake the alligators called **SPECTACLED CAIMANS** and join the **WATER OPOSSUM** with a fish in its mouth. It is the only marsupial—mammal with a pouch for its babies—that lives in water, and its pouch is watertight.

☞ Quick! Duck away from the **VAMPIRE BAT**. It feeds on blood and lands so softly that you may not feel it if it lands on you.

☞ Say hello to the **GIANT ARMADILLO** digging for worms and wearing more armor than any other mammal. It has been on Earth for 95 million years. Climb up and rest beside the spotted **JAGUAR**, the largest wildcat in the Americas.

☞ SEEK THE MAGIC CRYSTAL

27

THE HIMALAYAS

You are high in the Himalaya Mountains in Asia. Mount Everest, the tallest mountain in the world, is nearby. Move slowly. There isn't much oxygen, so it is hard to breathe this far up.

◄-- THE ROUTE --►

☞ Find two **BLACK BEARS** standing to play. Sometimes they curl into a ball and roll downhill. Can you see white markings like moons on their chests? They are also known as moon bears.

☞ Say hello to two small **PIKA** watching from under the rocks. They look like guinea pigs but are related to rabbits.

☞ Follow the **BUTTERFLY** up the rocks to two **IBEX**, fighting with horns locked. These goats have toes at the back of their feet and suction pads to grip rocky surfaces.

☞ Jump aross the stream to three **PHEASANTS** on the left. Then climb the rocks past the leaping ibex to the wild goat with spiraling horns and a long shaggy mane. It is a **MARKHOR** and its horns are 4 ft long.

☞ Look up! A **LAMMERGEIER** has just dropped a bone. This vulture drops bones to break them, then dives down and scoops up the marrow with its hooked beak.

☞ Swoop down past the vultures and stop by the tall monkey sitting on a rock. It is a **HIMALAYAN LANGUR.** Some people think it may also be the abominable snowman.

☞ Tired and cold? Ask two wild **YAK** for a ride. They are the largest mammals in these mountains.

☞ Now jump across the rocks with the **SNOW LEOPARD**. It moves very fast, using its bushy tail for balance. Don't expect it to roar like most big cats do. It can't.

☞ SEEK THE MAGIC CRYSTAL

THE ANDES

You are high in the Andes Mountains in South America. The air is thin and it is hard to breathe. A strong wind is blowing.

◄-- THE ROUTE --►

☞ It is dark overhead. **CONDORS**, the largest birds of prey in the world, are blocking out the light with their 10 ft wingspan. They can glide for over 55 miles without flapping their wings.

☞ Sprint along with the herd of **VICUÑA**, who are related to camels. Their wool is so fine that it used to be kept for Inca royalty only.

☞ Pass the **MOUNTAIN TAPIR**, who looks like a pig with a long snout, and snuggle under the rocks with three **GUINEA PIGS**. The Incas kept them as pets and bred them for food.

☞ Climb down to the small gray **CHINCHILLA**, watching two friends leap over rocks with their strong back legs. Soft, silky fur keeps these rodents warm in the cold mountains.

☞ Can you see baby **DARWIN'S FROGS** leaping from the mouth of their father? He looks after them in his throat until they are ready to look after themselves.

☞ Say hello to the **FLICKER** woodpecker and the **LIZARD**. Move on to the mountain lion, or **PUMA**. It doesn't roar like the true big cats, but it loves to purr.

☞ Hungry? Join the **HUMMINGBIRD** searching for nectar. It hovers in one place, beating its wings up to 80 times a second, and is the only bird in the world that can fly backward.

☞ Tired? Climb up to the tree nest and find the **SPECTACLED BEAR**. It has white fur around its eyes and is the only bear that lives in South America.

☞ SEEK THE MAGIC CRYSTAL

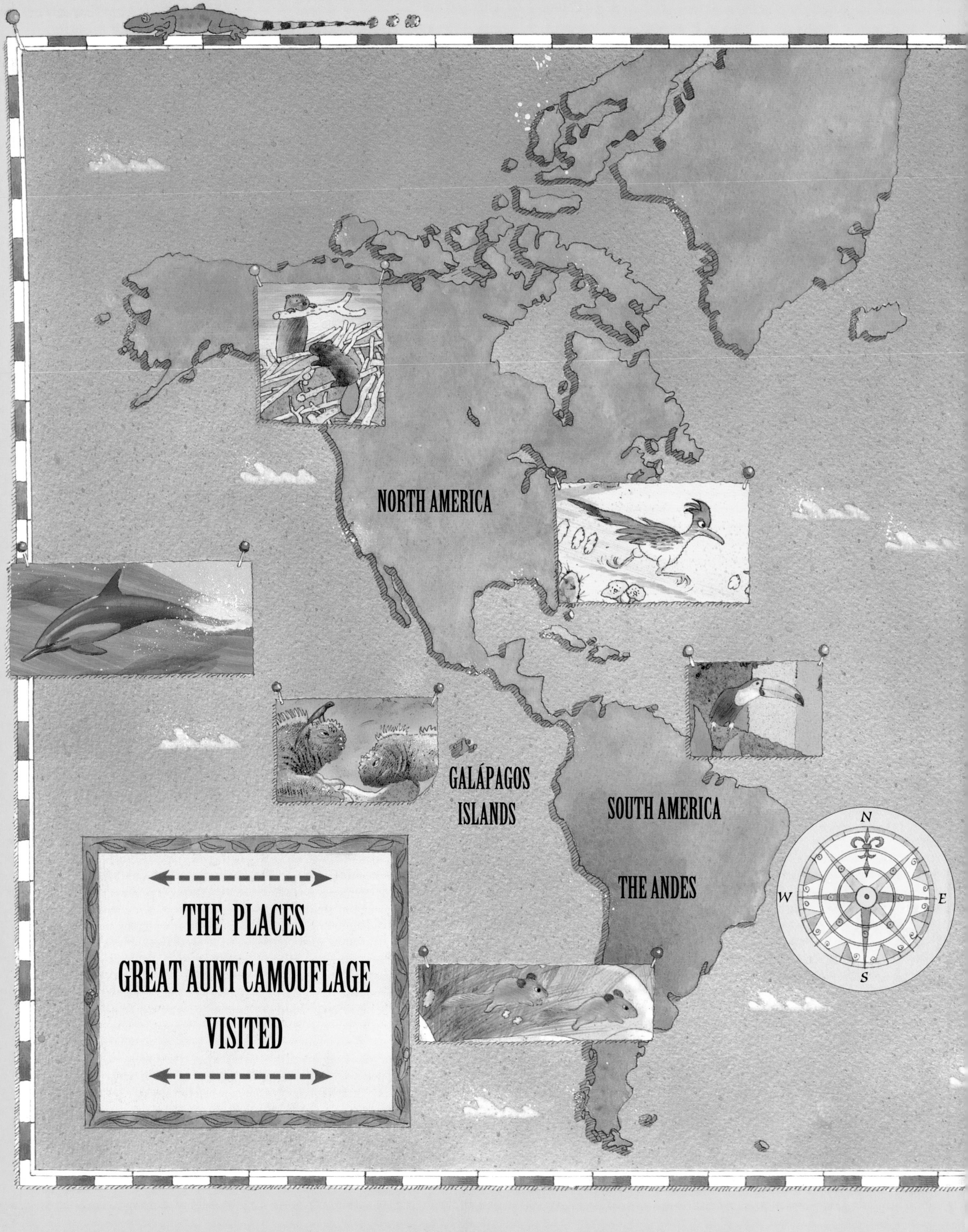

NORTH AMERICA

GALÁPAGOS
ISLANDS

SOUTH AMERICA

THE ANDES

THE PLACES
GREAT AUNT CAMOUFLAGE
VISITED

N

W   E

S